Adolf Hitler: Faces of a Dictator

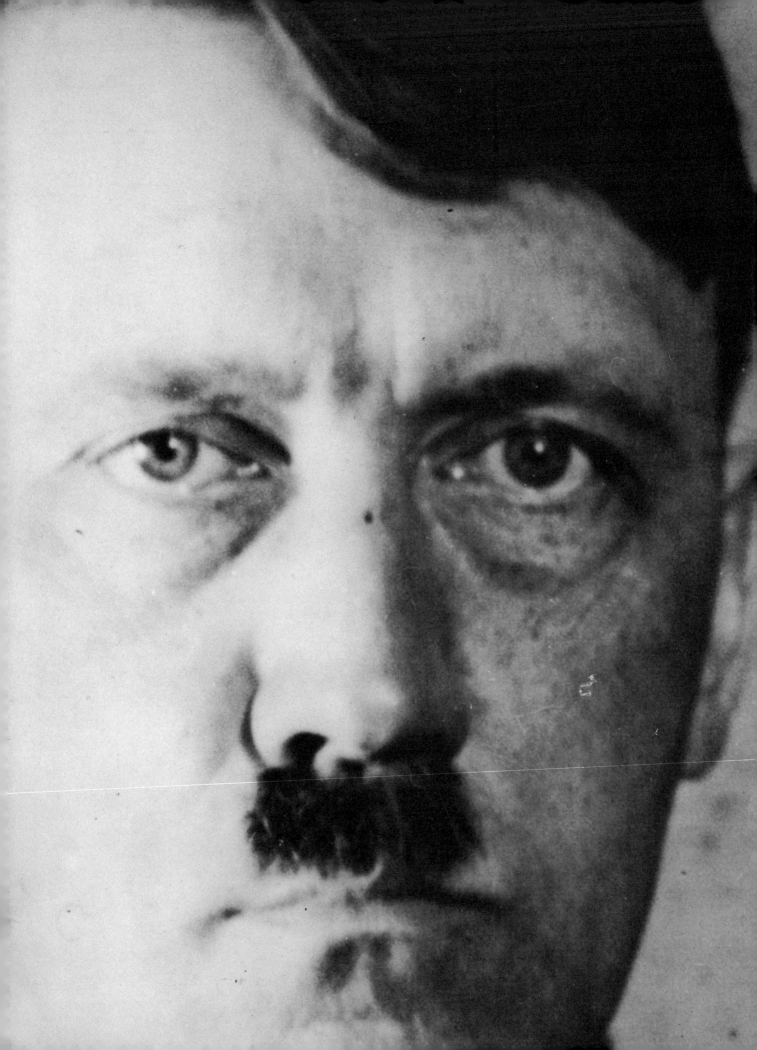

Photographs from the Heinrich Hoffmann Archives

ADOLF HITLER

FACES OF A DICTATOR

Text and Captions by Jochen von Lang

With an Introduction by Constantine FitzGibbon

Harcourt, Brace & World, Inc., New York

Heinrich Hoffmann, Hitler's official photographer, took two and a half million photographs of the Führer of the Third Reich. Most of them were never published, Hitler having forbidden their publication.

Hoffmann's father was official court photographer to the Bavarian royal house, and it was as his apprentice that the son took his own first photographs. After a further apprenticeship in Switzerland and England—in London he studied with the most eminent of contemporary European photographers, E. O. Hoppe—he opened his own studio in Munich in 1909, specializing in political photo reporting. His photographs of Kaiser Wilhelm II and King Edward VII were printed by news media throughout the world.

In 1922 an American press service commissioned him to take the picture of an obscure Bavarian political figure, Adolf Hitler, thus leading fortuitously to a permanent relationship between the two men. Hoffmann became Hitler's official photographer at the beginning of Hitler's political career. He was the only one permitted to photograph the Führer in public and in private. Accompanying Hitler from 1922 to 1945, he assembled a unique sequence of pictures, preserved in the Zeitgeschichtliches Bildarchiv, an archive administered, after Heinrich Hoffmann's death in 1957, by his son.

All the photographs in this volume are taken from this archive, and many of them are released for the first time for publication here. Rather than attempting chronological comprehensiveness, the sequence aims to underline the physiological characteristics of the dictator in his rise from obscurity to absolute power and in his subsequent decline and fall.

Introduction

Only the greatest artists, and not all of them, have succeeded in avoiding a certain quality that verges on the insipid when portraying the Saints and the Holy Family. In their attempts to visualize absolute goodness the painters not infrequently deprive the Apostles of their absolute and essential humanity: to show the utter courage and devotion of martyrdom, at times they make Saint Sebastian, though as full of arrows as a pincushion is of pins, seem almost to simper in his torment. For such supreme qualities are extremely hard to portray visually, harder than in words and far harder than in music. The physical man in whom the absolute virtues are believed to be incarnate will keep getting in the way. And unless the painter's own devotion is total, as in a Fra Angelico, he must suspect, as we all do and as Jean Racine remarked, that a man is never altogether good nor altogether bad. Perhaps this is the sound reason for Jewish and Moslem prohibitions in the plastic arts.

If this is true of the portrayal of virtue, it is at least as true in the representation of vice. There are innumerable excellent and revealing portraits of weak, foolish, ugly, unkind men and women, very few of real monsters or even of situations truly monstrous within the human framework of life. The great religious artists seldom attempted a Judas Iscariot and never, I think, successfully. Their scenes of hell, devils with pitchforks and so on, are either mere allegories or, when emotionally successful, verge away from the human to the surreal as with Carpaccio or Hieronymus Bosch. Perhaps Goya came closest to painting absolute evil in human terms, but even his foulest torturers, his most drunken brigands and soldiers, preserve a glint of humanity and are, therefore, not "altogether bad."

If this is so of the most exquisite and sensitive artists throughout the ages, it is even more so of the photographers who practiced their art or craft since its invention in the last century. And when those photographers are, as it were, court photographers the character of the monarch they serve can and will be easily traduced: the glint of greed in the eye, the callous line of the lips replaced by kinder and more attractive emotions. Stalin, one of the great monsters, was shown to the world by his court photographers as the solid, pipe-smoking, smiling, grandchild-on-knee Uncle Joe who won, for a while, the hearts of the American and British publics. And in this book we see, almost man to man, almost face to face, the vilest tyrant of our century, the face of a man who must certainly be considered for the title of the most evil man who has ever lived. Such is hardly the impression that one would get from Hoffmann's photographs, even those that his wicked "monarch" regarded as unsuitable for publication.

Nor is this vast difference between the man's appearance and his spiritual reality due solely to the skill of his court photographer. During the last thirty-odd years I have had occasion, as a journalist or in some other capacity, to meet a number of political figures whom I loathe, despise, or fear— including the subject of these photographs. I have, almost without exception, found these greater or lesser monsters endued with a considerable degree of charm and intelligence. (But then, I was never in their power, let alone an object of their vengeance.) Indeed, they had clearly needed a measure of charm and intelligence to get where they had got. Nor, I think, am I particularly gullible. Certainly so far as Hitler goes, far shrewder, older, and more experienced men than I were also impressed. David Lloyd George was but one among many.

I have told the story of my sole meeting with Hitler elsewhere, but believe that it is worth retelling here. It was in Munich, in 1936, when I was seventeen, an art student, thought I was a Communist, hated Nazism, its leader and all his works, and was, briefly, a passionate opera-goer. In Munich in those days students could purchase, for one mark, any theater seats still unsold a few minutes before the rise of the curtain. I queued up almost every night and was frequently in luck. The unsold seats that came to us were usually the best and most expensive in the house. The royal box, for instance, was empty most evenings.

I was seated in it one night, together with a dozen or so other students, all unknown to me, waiting for the lights to dim, when two gigantic S.S. men walked in. "All out!" they ordered. "Führer's coming!" We trooped out, into a sort of drawing room behind the royal box, where we came face to face with him and his entourage coming in. We fell back against the side walls in order that they might pass, but he stopped and, therefore, his companions stopped behind him. He apologized for turning us out of the box and said that there would be seats for us in the stalls below or maybe at the next performance of this particular opera. He then shook us each by the hand and inquired our names. When he came to me, and realized that I was a foreigner, he asked me what I was studying in Munich. I told him. He made some remarks, which I believe were part of his limited repertoire of small talk, about the artist's life, how it is the best, how he wished it could have been his. Then he passed on. I believe my astonishment would have been considerably less had he actually revealed horns, a tail, and cloven hoofs.

This charming, courteous, considerate man had *at that time* scores of thousands of his compatriots locked up in camps, where, with his full knowledge and approval, they were being tortured and murdered: *at that time* he was undoubtedly planning, if only in his own mind and with his closest party comrades, the war that was to cost fifty million lives; long before then he had already decided on the extermination of the Jews. Yet none of this appeared on his face, any more than it does in the pictures in this book. Any man who can detect, from them, the monstrosity of Hitler's character and will is either a clairvoyant or is seeing what he wishes to see.

Hannah Arendt has written, *à propos* the genocide Eichmann, of how on trial he revealed the horrible vacuum within himself, the mediocrity of mind and utter orthodoxy of views (Nazi views, of course) that made him the murderous mirror-image of the *Spiessbürger, petit-bourgeois, Bouvard et Pécuchet* type of bore who justifies all Bohemian rebellion and intellectual nonconformity. Hitler has been described as an "armed Bohemian," and insofar as he rejected all bourgeois morality, this is not inaccurate. But far more does it seem to me that in him these qualities of Eichmann's reached and were implemented in truly daemonic proportions.

His conversation, to judge not only from the reports of his intimates but also from his recorded *Table Talk*, was an almost incredibly boring monologue, matched only by his intellectual arrogance in ordering that this interminable string of flat remarks, boasts, and snippets of often incorrect information be recorded for all posterity. The taste of this "artist" was execrable, even by politicians' standards, as his collections of pictures, the furnishings of his palaces, and his plans for rebuilding postwar Germany all show. He dressed badly, ate worse, and his table manners appear to have been disgusting as he crouched over his plate shoveling his vegetarian muck into his mouth. He drank nothing, but increasingly permitted his quack physicians to pump him full of noxious sedatives and stimulants. He had no close friends, or, rather one, Ernst Röhm, whom he murdered in June of

1934. His disloyalty to his comrades, to his soldiers, and ultimately to the German people even exceeded that of Napoleon Bonaparte to his people and his country. Only toward Mussolini, in the Italian dictator's ruin, for which they were both directly responsible, did the German dictator preserve a measure of honesty and loyalty. His sex life was squalid, boring, and small. Some think that he contracted syphilis from a Viennese prostitute in his youth, which in its tertiary form produced Parkinson's disease toward the end of his life. His love affair with his niece and her suicide in his Munich flat are scarcely romantic or edifying. His liaison with Eva Braun, on the other hand, seems comparatively healthy until the end. But if a man loves a woman he will hardly marry her at the last moment merely in order that she commit suicide when his career is over. If he loved her, it was much as he loved his German sheep dog, Blondi. And at the end Blondi was also murdered by the order of his loving master.

Why, we may well wonder, are we still so interested, a quarter of a century later, in this boring, squalid, uncouth monster? Why are you reading this? Indeed, why am I writing it? His enormously evil career has been documented *ad nauseam* in books both scholarly and popular. Yet we hope that by examining his features we may, somehow, come to understand more about the man himself. Why such further enlightenment about the man seems to me unlikely from such a source, I have already explained. Nevertheless, I pored over these photographs with the greatest possible interest, though I did not really believe that they could provide any sort of clue, nor even that a clue was needed. Yet I still suspect that I may have more understanding of his relationship with Eva Braun by comparing pictures 84 and 96 in this book, of his dog Blondi by looking at 94, even perhaps of the man in ruins after the assassination attempt, sick and drugged and, as he thought, betrayed, by comparing 88 with some of Hoffmann's earlier portraits. One suspects one's own judgment, yet one looks. Why?

The answer is complex, not flattering, and intimately connected with Hitler's relations to our world both as man and as symbol. One reason for our interest is, quite simply, the enormity of his infamy, the numerical enormity which is based in his case on the enormous power he briefly enjoyed. (And for what other reasons than a fascination with power, even reflected power, do the newspapers write about Mrs. Richard Nixon or Mrs. Harold Wilson?) Crime also fascinates, and in direct geometric proportion, it seems, to its enormity. Many a poor prostitute has been murdered by many a poor psychopath. These murders rate a half-inch in the yellow press, but quite serious writers still write whole books about Jack the Ripper for the simple reason that he murdered a dozen or so in a particularly disgusting manner. We, the public, are fascinated snobbishly by numbers and morbidly by depravity. If Hitler was the most evil man who ever lived, with more murders on his score card than perhaps any other monster, then quite simply we want to see what this monster looked like, to hear what he had for breakfast. In the freak show of history he is one of the top freaks. People queue up for freak shows.

Next, he used this enormous power principally for the infliction of pain and misery. Since power produces such strong emotions—which may be those of repulsion, attraction, and in extreme cases fascination—the more absolute the power the stronger the response. And in view of the divergence between the intellect and the emotions, the violence of the response has little connection with the manner in which power is exercised. On the sexual level lust and love are often, and often rightly, confused. Once politics, war, even mass murder are employed with the skill of our twentieth-century tyrants to canalize this basic confusion in the tyrants' own interests, the lust for power can quite easily be transformed into the love of tyrants. And since for most people the ultimate in lust, after satiety, is the further infliction of personality through cruelty, the real monsters become, at second hand, the realization of fantasy.

At the intellectual level this form of self-gratification is denied by almost all decent people. The gentle liberal, advocating pacifism perhaps and a mild form of socialism certainly, did not "approve" of Stalin's massacre of the kulaks or the purges that followed and the massacre of the old Bolsheviks: he even denied, against all the evidence, that these atrocities were going on; yet he wallowed, dishonestly, in his adoration of total power and therefore adored the Soviet Union, and rationalized his self-indulgence in power fantasies as a hatred of the power apparatus in Nazi Germany. The violence of emotion remained to warm their libido. The gentle liberal needs, perhaps more than most men, his vicarious "thrills." Similarly, many men, in Britain in 1939 and in the United States in 1941, though consciously and honestly avowed pacifists, felt an immense relief when at last they were allowed to go to war, to dress up in uniform and thus lose part of their conscious and honest identity, to kill the enemy, perhaps any enemy.

To these basic urges Hitler is still a figure of absorbing interest, repulsive as he may be in every respect to those who so respond. Milton loved God, or so he thought, but Satan remains the hero of *Paradise Lost*, made even more heroic by every black and damning line that Milton wrote.

Shortly after Hitler's death, indeed in 1945, Dr. Max Picard (1888–1965), a German writer on physiognomics, philosophy, and art who had moved to Switzerland in the early 1930's, published a book called *Hitler in uns selbst*, published in America two years later with the title *Hitler in Our Selves*, but not so far published in England. Its basic thesis is that Hitler was the symbol of mass-man, of the urban product of industrialization. In industrial societies, the Professor argues, values have become atrophied to a point at which all sensations become equivalent. In those days before television, he gave radio as an example, though TV would be an even more effective one. Mass-man, according to him, will listen with imperturbable interest or lack of interest to a "program" split into fifteen-minute slices of pop music, the weather forecast, the news of an earthquake in Brazil and of a film star's divorce, a Beethoven quartet, an analysis of the economic situation, a comedian telling semidirty jokes, a football game, a poetry reading, the description of a jail break, and so on. The whole external world is reduced by the mass media, on which of course mass-man's conversations with his peers is based almost exclusively, to the status of stale *hors d'oeuvres*, and human nature being what it is, the only main course left is violence, at the gentlest level the violence of industrial dispute and of political protest, but more deliciously the violence of war. And when war itself becomes nothing more for the viewer or listener than an apparently perpetual *fait divers* of victory and defeat, then gamier meat is desired, perhaps genocide, first, eventually the destruction of the planet.

Love needs a fruitful soil in which to flourish: hatred can thrive in a vacuum. Ghosts presumably do best in an empty, preferably a ruined, house. Hitler's was an empty, at the end a ruined, mind, filled with ghouls and spooks and hag-ridden with horrors both of his imagination and of his creation. It was thus that he became, and has remained, a symbolic and even a "heroic" figure for a civilization that has denied God, the gods, now the arts, respect for humanity, love of nature, even and increasingly the enjoyment of pleasure, as mankind sinks into this new, dark, technological age whose first truly spectacular achievement was the extermination camp at Auschwitz.

This ghastly, and I hope exaggerated, view of the world was epitomized in the mind that was housed within the body here portrayed. That is why he appealed to so many Germans of his generation, and that is why he is still of interest to us.

CONSTANTINE FITZGIBBON

Adolf Hitler: Faces of a Dictator

On January 22, 1933, the Nazis held demonstrations in the German capital, Berlin. Adolf Hitler, leader of the Brown Shirts, the strongest party in Germany, spoke these words at the tomb of S.A. man Horst Wessel: "Even when centuries have gone by, when the great city of Berlin is in ruins, the greatest German movement of liberation and its singer will still be remembered!"

A week later, Hitler was Chancellor of the Reich and assumed power in Germany. For twelve years the Germans kept singing the Horst Wessel song, "Hold High the Flag," as a second national anthem. On April 30, 1945, Hitler committed suicide in the ruins of Berlin. The Second World War, which he started and which ended for Germany with unconditional surrender, cost the world fifty million human lives.

Adolf Hitler was born in the small Austrian border town of Braunau on the Inn on April 20, 1889. He was the fourth child of Klara and Alois Hitler. His father, who was a customs official, was illegitimate and had borne the name of his mother, Schicklgruber, until his thirty-ninth year, when he changed it to that of his father, Hitler, on confirmation of his paternity. Alois Hitler died in 1903 during his son's thirteenth year. He had hoped that Adolf would become an official like himself, but his son's poor performance at school prevented this. Hitler had to leave high school in 1905 without having graduated, and, supported by his mother, he loafed for two years. In 1907 he applied for admission to the Viennese Academy of Fine Arts to become a painter, but his drawings were unsatisfactory and he failed to gain admittance there, as well as to the School of Architecture.

In February, 1908, two months after the death of his mother, Hitler moved from Linz to Vienna, where he lived on an orphan's pension which he supplemented with money he earned painting picture postcards. There he began to interest himself in politics: he became an anti-Semite, denounced Marxism, and turned against democracy. He looked forward to the fall of the Habsburg monarchy, which he derided as the "Czech State," and refused to do his military service. His dream was the union of Austria and Germany.

In 1913 he fled to Germany to evade military service. The Austrian police traced him to Munich and on February 5, 1914, brought him before the service board in Salzburg. There, he was exempted from military service as physically unfit and declared unable to bear arms.

At the start of the First World War, Hitler enlisted as a volunteer and went to the Western front with the Bavarian Infantry Regiment, List. On December 2, 1914, he was awarded the Order of the Iron Cross 2nd Class. In August, 1918, the Iron Cross 1st Class, for outstanding bravery, was conferred on him. Temporarily blinded by gas, Corporal Hitler witnessed the revolution and the collapse of the German Empire in the Military Hospital in Pasewalk.

In his book *Mein Kampf* he later put the responsibility for the lost war on the Jews and Marxists: "Emperor Wilhelm II was the first German Emperor who held out his hand in reconciliation to the leaders of Marxism, unaware that scoundrels are without honor. While they were still grasping the Emperor's hand in their own, they were groping with the other for the knife. With the Jew you cannot negotiate, there is only the harsh either/or."

At the end of 1918, Hitler was released from the hospital and he returned to Bavaria, determined to enter politics. Germany was then in the throes of revolution, with Friedrich Ebert, the Social Democrat and head of the provisional government, trying to re-establish peace and order. On January 5, 1919, a Munich railroad mechanic, Anton Drexler, founded the German Workers' Party. "Free from foreign influence," it was to be a rival to the Marxist labor movement. A Red Workers' Republic was proclaimed in Bavaria on April 7, 1919, but the rebellion was crushed three weeks later by the German Army with the collaboration of a volunteer corps. The unrest throughout Germany continued.

On June 28, 1919, the German government signed the Versailles Peace Treaty. On September 16, 1919, four days after having attended a rally of the German Workers' Party, Adolf Hitler joined the party: his membership number was 555; the numbering, however, had started at 501. He rose rapidly, and on February 24, 1920, Hitler, by then propaganda speaker of the party, proclaimed the party program at the Munich Hofbräuhaus and changed its name to the National Socialist German Workers' Party (NSDAP). The following year, on June 29, he became the Party chairman, with dictatorial authority.

In January, 1922, the NSDAP numbered 6,000 registered members and in November it was suspended for the first time by the Social Democratic government in Prussia. Saxony, Thuringia, Hamburg, and other states followed suit. Hitler countered these measures in a Munich assembly: "The Marxists think: 'And if you don't want to be my brother, I'll crack your skull.' Our slogan is: 'And if you don't want to be a German, I'll crack your skull.'"

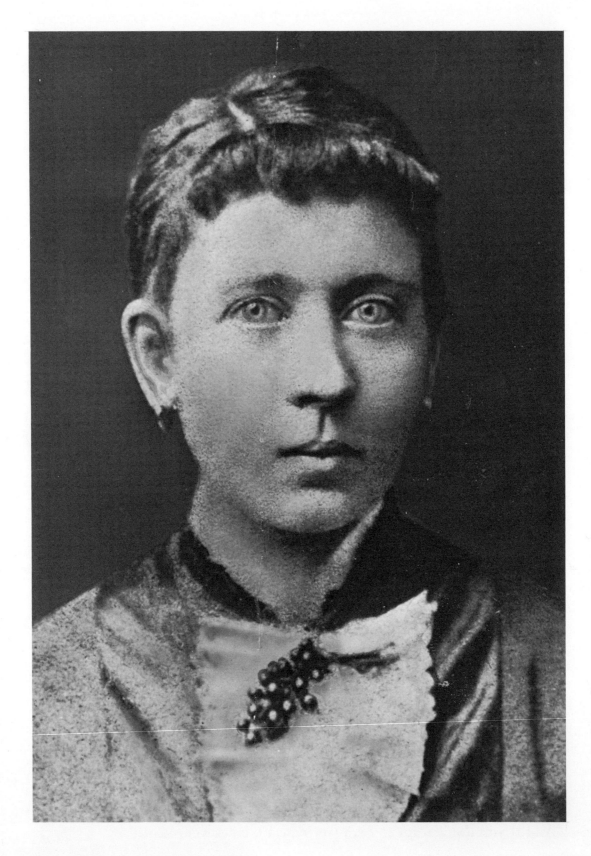

1 / Klara Hitler, Adolf Hitler's mother

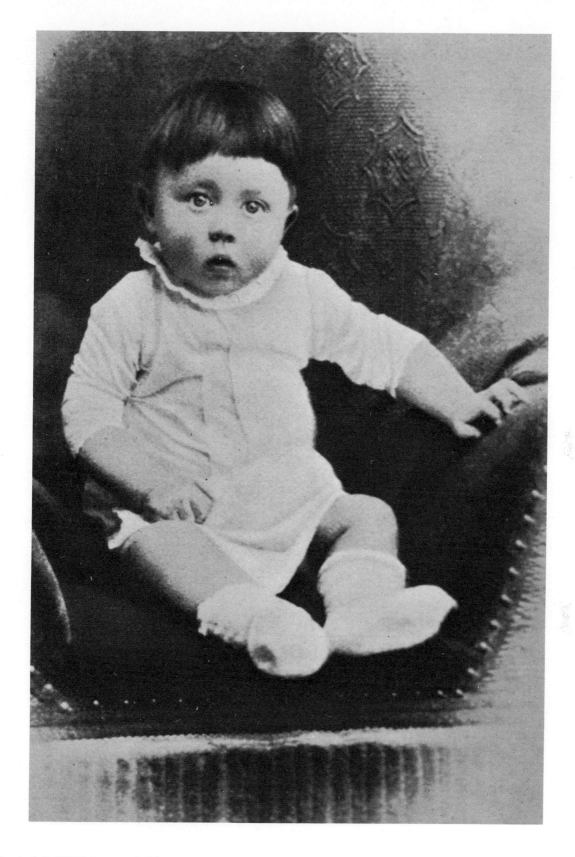

2 / Adolf Hitler as child

3 / Chancellor Adolf Hitler

4 / Hitler's father, Alois Hitler

5 / 1899: Ten-year-old Adolf Hitler (*upper row, center*) as pupil in the elementary school in Leonding/Linz

6 / Hitler, as prisoner in Landsberg Fortress

7 / Drawing of Hitler at sixteen by a fellow student

8 / 1914:
Mobilization in Germany.
On Odeon Square
in Munich,
Hitler and
Bavarian patriots sing
the "Watch on the Rhine"

9 / November 4, 1923:
Hitler, with Dr. Weber,
leader of the
"Volunteer Corps Oberland,"
at his right,
watches
the *Freikorps* marching by.
At Hitler's left,
Alfred Rosenberg,
editor-in-chief of
the *Völkische Beobachter*
(the party paper),
1941 Reich Minister for the
occupied Eastern territories;
executed 1946 in
Nuremberg

10 / February 24, 1924: Hitler and his fellow conspirators on trial for high treason in front of the People's Court, Munich.

Left to right: **Pernet, Dr. Weber, Dr. Frick, Kriebel, Ludendorff, Hitler, Brückner, Röhm, Wagner**

11 / Hitler practicing oratorical gestures before the camera of
photographer Heinrich Hoffmann

In 1923 dissatisfaction among the German population reached its peak and inflation its climax. On November 1 the value of the dollar was 130 billion Reichsmarks. Unrest continued to shake the country, and in several parts of Germany, notably in Bavaria, secession from the Reich was contemplated.

Hitler considered this the auspicious moment to seize power. On November 8 he proclaimed "the national revolution" in a Munich beer hall, the Bürgerbräukeller, and appointed himself Chancellor of the Reich. He intended to march on Berlin with his followers and there take over governmental powers. But the morning after, the Bavarian provincial police halted the demonstration march of the National Socialists at Munich's Feldherrnhalle. Hitler's first attempt to assume power had miscarried.

The Party, whose membership had meanwhile risen to 55,787, was suspended, and Hitler, together with his co-conspirators, was brought to trial on February 24, 1924.

General Otto von Lossow, Commander in Chief of the Reichswehr in Bavaria, testified before the People's Court: "Hitler looks upon himself as the German Mussolini, and his followers term him the German Messiah.

"The well-known overwhelming and persuasive rhetoric of Hitler carried me away at first. But the more often I heard him the less this first impression was confirmed. I noticed that his long speeches were repetitive. While one part of his exposition was self-evident to any national-minded German, the other part demonstrated that Hitler completely lacked any sense of reality and of discrimination as to what is possible and feasible."

Hitler said in his final summing up: "Whoever is born to be a dictator is not persuaded but exerts his own will; he is not pushed, he pushes himself to the forefront. . . . Whoever feels himself called to govern a people does not have the right to say: 'I will collaborate if you want me and seek me out.' It is his duty to act on his own."

The Court condemned Hitler and three of his fellow conspirators, Pohner, Kriebel, and Dr. Weber, to five years' detention in the Landsberg Fortress. Other conspirators were each sentenced to one year and three months and immediately released. Field Marshal Erich Ludendorff, who had participated in the demonstration march, was acquitted.

During his detention at Landsberg Fortress, Hitler wrote the first volume of *Mein Kampf*.

The Bavarian government considered freeing Hitler on parole after thirteen months' detention, on the grounds of "good behavior." The Bavarian police, in a report of September 22, 1924, warned against it: "As soon as he is released, Hitler, owing to his energy, will again be the driving force of renewed and serious public unrest and will be a threat to the security of the state. Hitler will resume his political activities, and the hope of the nationalists and populists that he will succeed in overcoming the present strife among the semimilitary associations will come true."

Despite this warning, Hitler was released on December 20, 1924. He visited the Bavarian Premier, Dr. Heinrich Held, and promised to confine his political activity within the framework of legality. Held thereupon rescinded the suspension of the National Socialist Party and permitted the reappearance of the party organ, *Völkische Beobachter*. Held commented after Hitler's visit: "The beast is tamed, now we can loosen the fetters." On February 27, 1925, at the reinstatement of the National Socialist Party, Hitler proclaimed in the Bürgerbräukeller: "Either our enemy steps over our corpses or we step over his."

The Bavarian government countered Hitler's provocative speeches against the democratic order by barring him from public speaking. Other German states followed suit, and for a time Hitler was free to speak only in Württemberg, Thuringia, Braunschweig, and Mecklenburg-Schwerin.

On the following two pages:

12 / 1925: Released from prison, Hitler visits a Bavarian local party group

13 / Hitler talking to
Captain Franz Pfeffer von Salomon,
Chief of the S.A. 1926–1930.
In the background,
Hitler's secretary, Rudolf Hess

14 / Hitler at rally

At right:

15 / Orator's histrionics

16 / Party convention

17 / Hitler (wearing hat), in discussion with party faithfuls
at the Café Heck in Munich's Hofgarten

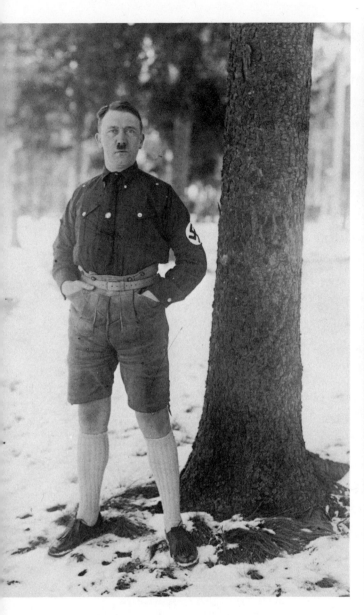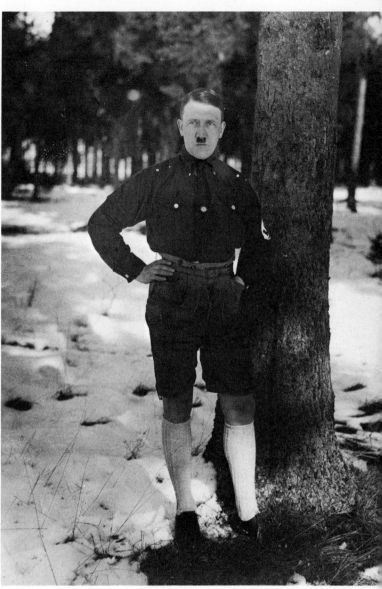

18 / Hitler in Bavarian national costume posing for cameraman
Heinrich Hoffmann

Friedrich Ebert, the first President of the German Republic, died on February 28, 1925. Paul von Hindenburg, Field Marshal and victor over the Russians in the Battle of Tannenberg, was elected as his successor. Hitler expected preferential treatment for the right-wing parties from the monarchist Hindenburg, but the Field Marshal respected the democratic constitution of the Weimar Republic. The young Republic gained stability. The currency was finally stabilized, the economy revived, and the standard of living rose. The German people began to turn away from political radicalism. This was an unpromising starting point for Hitler and his road to power. In the few provinces in which he was free to speak, he went canvassing from village to village, beseeching his followers: "All the parties and public opinion are against us. But this is the premise, I might say the mathematically calculable reason, for the future victory of our movement. . . . As long as we are a radical movement, as long as we are outlawed by public opinion, as long as the prevailing conditions in the state are against us, we shall continue to attract the most valuable human material, even in times in which, as the saying goes, all arguments of human reason speak against us." Hitler continued to foment mistrust among the Germans. The First World War, he alleged, was the consequence of a universal conspiracy against Germany. It was lost because Marxists and Jews had planned Germany's defeat. The Versailles Peace Treaty was a shameful instrument intended to enslave the Germans forever. The leaders of the Weimar Republic were delivering Germany to its enemies.

An assistant to the U.S. military attaché in Germany, Captain Truman Smith, listening to Hitler's speeches in Munich, reported to his government as early as 1922: "Hitler's ability to sway a mass meeting is uncanny."

For the time being, Hitler and his party played only a marginal role in German politics. In the Reichstag, the German Parliament, the NSDAP's 14 deputies were an insignificant minority among 493 deputies. To get himself and his party into the limelight, Hitler decided to do something spectacular. The referendum concerning compensation for German princes gave him the desired opportunity. He backed the restitution of the property of German princes confiscated in 1918, and unintentionally brought about a crisis within his own party.

The North German party members under the leadership of the brothers Gregor and Otto Strasser favored nationalization and accused Hitler of betraying socialism and of bribery by the princes. Party member Dr. Joseph Goebbels, subsequently Hitler's Minister of Propaganda, demanded: "In view of these circumstances I move that the petty bourgeois, Adolf Hitler, be expelled from the party."

Bernhard Rust, later Hitler's Minister of Education, and a suicide at the war's end, also protested: "National Socialists are free men and democrats. They do not acknowledge a pope who might consider himself infallible."

The North German party leaders decided to develop their own party program and to disassociate themselves from Hitler and his Munich movement.

Hitler countered this by calling a meeting of the entire party in Bamberg, at which the National Socialists cast their vote against the expropriation of the princes. Goebbels admitted that the dissidents were in error. There was only one possibility: to follow Hitler.

In the parliamentary elections of May 20, 1928, the National Socialists lost two of their seats. Only twelve deputies were left to represent the party in Parliament, and Hitler feared the total disintegration of the party. In spite of his fears, however, he pretended self-assurance and attacked the German government in a speech in Weimar shortly after the elections: "You say: we are here to stay, at all costs. I say: we will beat you, you can count on that."

With the exception of his handful of followers, nobody took the man from Braunau seriously. For the government, as for the majority of Germans, he was the outsider from Bavaria.

19 / Weimar, 1926:
Hitler,
watching his adherents
march past
the Hotel Elephant,
raising his arm in the
"German salute"

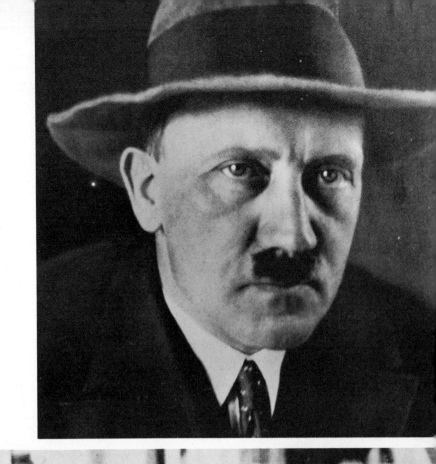

20 / Hitler and Rudolf Hess, his secretary, who on Hitler's
assumption of power became his party deputy. On May 10, 1941,
Hess, on his own initiative, flew to Scotland as peace mediator.
Since then imprisoned

21 / Nuremberg Party Rally 1927: Hitler is enthusiastically acclaimed
(*foreground left,* Julius Streicher, executed 1946 in Nuremberg)

At right:

23 / Hitler's hand

22 / Hitler at the funeral of an S.A. man killed by political opponents, with General Heinemann, President of the Party Court (*left*), and Rudolf Hess

24 / 1928: Hitler addresses the Party Board.
Left to right: Rosenberg, editor-in-chief of the party newspaper
(with clasped hands); Party Judge Buch; Treasurer Schwarz; Hitler;

Gregor Strasser, Hitler's strongest opponent in the party; Himmler, deputy propaganda chief, later Commander of the bodyguard corps S.S. (Schutz-Staffel) and in charge of concentration camps

25 / Respite during a journey across Germany. Next to Hitler,
Magda Goebbels, wife of the subsequent Propaganda Minister

At right:

26 / Hitler relaxing among his intimates:
Top, left to right: Goebbels,
Frau Goebbels, Julius Schaub,
Hitler's aide, Hitler, Frau Hoffmann,
Secretary Johanna Wolff

27 / Vacation on Tegernsee. Hitler steering the motorboat
of party publisher Müller

Finally, in February, 1929, Hitler saw the chance he had been waiting for.

Under the chairmanship of an American, Owen D. Young, German reparations payments were discussed in Paris. The conference came to the following decision: Germany was to make reparations payments for a period of 59 years, to a total of 1.2 billion gold marks. Since it presented a considerable improvement over earlier demands of the victors, this proposal was welcomed by the German Foreign Minister, Gustav Stresemann. Stresemann hoped to reduce payments still further in future negotiations and finally to arrive at their complete cancellation. But overnight, Stresemann, who had brought about the reconciliation of Germany with France and Germany's entry into the League of Nations, was branded as a traitor by all the right-wing politicians. Hitler had found his slogan: "You will be slaves until 1988."

When it came to a plebiscite, he allied himself with the German Nationalists (Deutschnationale Volkspartei) and their leader, the industrialist Alfred Hugenberg, who controlled a large sector of the German bourgeois press. From now on, Hugenberg's papers supported Hitler, and made him a national figure. His party grew: in the summer of 1929, the National Socialist Party had 120,000 registered members, by the end of the year 178,000; in the spring of 1930, it had grown to nearly 210,000, and nine months later to almost 400,000.

The world-wide economic crisis which started at the end of 1929 again brought misery to the Germans. Throughout the years the number of unemployed rose from 3 million to 6.2 million and created another boon for Hitler's propaganda. He knew how to make use of it. In the autumn of 1930 the government published a white paper documenting the subversiveness of the National Socialist Party, but Hitler's party polled 107 seats in the parliamentary elections. The outsiders of 1928 had become the second-largest party in Germany.

Testifying shortly after the parliamentary elections, Hitler declared before the German Federal Court in Leipzig that his party would assume power only by legal means.

At a meeting of party executives, however, he gave his directions for the future seizure of power: "First, our people must be freed from disastrous internationalism, and deliberately and systematically trained to fanatical nationalism. . . . Secondly, by educating our people to fight against the madness of democracy and again to understand the necessity of authority and leadership, we will tear them away from the nonsense of parliamentarianism. Thirdly, by liberating the people from their pitiful belief in international reconciliation, world peace, the League of Nations, and international solidarity, we shall destroy these ideas. There is only one right in the world, and that is the right conferred by one's own might."

In the province of Braunschweig, where the Minister of the Interior was a party member, Hitler was appointed to a high office in the civil service in early 1932. This conferred on him German citizenship and removed the last barrier to his political career. In the parliamentary elections of July 31, 1932, the National Socialists won 230 seats, which made them the strongest party in Germany. Hitler was offered the post of Vice-Chancellor in a conservative government structure, but declined. He wanted nothing short of supreme power.

At this moment the economic crisis started to ebb and unemployment to decline. The Germans again withdrew from right-wing radicalism, and in the November elections Hitler's party lost 34 seats. For the first time Hitler gave way to despair: "Should the party ever disintegrate, I will put an end to myself with a pistol."

In mid-January, 1933, Hitler again staked everything on one card. Elections were to be held in the small government district of Lippe. As in the early days of his political career, he canvassed from village to village. Pitting himself against thirty competing parties, he pleaded for the trust of the voters. The National Socialists gained 18 per cent over the election results of the year before and were the uncontested victors. But even in Lippe they were unable to poll a clear majority.

28 / Hitler with Göring (*center*), who committed suicide in Nuremberg 1946, and with Röhm, liquidated by Hitler in 1934

29 / 1929: Hitler
at the Nuremberg
Party Rally

30 / Hitler
with party faithfuls:
Dr. Frick, later
Minister of the Interior,
executed in Nuremberg
1946;
Dr. Goebbels,
Propaganda Minister,
who committed suicide
with his wife in 1945,
killing also
his six children

31 / Hitler with Sauckel, District Leader of Thuringia (executed
in Nuremberg in 1946), at a Weimar election rally for Hermann Göring;
on August 30, 1932, Göring became President of the German Parliament

On the following two pages:

32 / 1935: Hitler as best man at the
wedding of Göring with actress Emmy Sonnemann

33 / May 1933:
President of the Republic
von Hindenburg
and
Chancellor Adolf Hitler

34 / Hitler
with actress and stage manager
Leni Riefenstahl

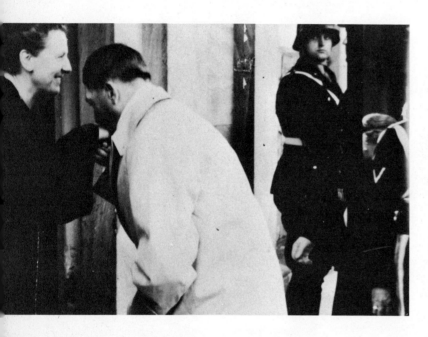

35 / With Winifred Wagner,
daughter-in-law of Richard Wagner

36 / With boxing champion
Max Schmeling and his wife,
the film actress Anny Ondra

37 / 1933: Hitler welcomes Vice-Chancellor Franz von Papen

39 / Hitler's niece, Geli Raubal, believed
to have been Hitler's mistress. She
committed suicide, shooting herself in
1931 in Hitler's Munich apartment

At left:

38 / Chancellor Hitler and Foreign Minister von Neurath
after a reception for foreign diplomats

40 / Hitler in formal dress

As a result of the Lippe elections the German Nationalist Party and their paramilitary organization, the Stahlhelm, decided to continue co-operating with the National Socialists. On January 28, 1933, Franz von Papen succeeded in persuading Field Marshal Hindenburg, President of the Weimar Republic, to offer Hitler the Chancellorship of the Reich, the top position he had been gambling for. Hindenburg evidently no longer remembered that, as recently as September, 1932, Hitler had said of the aged Field Marshal: "In one thing I am ahead of my greatest antagonist. The President is eighty-five years old, I am forty-three and in excellent health. . . . When I am eighty-five, Herr von Hindenburg will have long left the scene. It's our turn now."

On January 30, 1933, Hindenburg, overcoming his aversion to the "Corporal from Bohemia," as he disdainfully labeled Hitler, entrusted him with the formation of a new Cabinet consisting of National Socialists and Conservatives. Hitler, overriding the opposition of his conservative partners in the Cabinet, persuaded Hindenburg to dissolve Parliament and announce new elections for March 5. Hitler then used the interim period to curtail the freedom of his opponents.

When, on February 27, 1933, the Reichstag was set on fire, Hitler prevailed on President Hindenburg to suspend the constitutional order by decree "for the protection of the people and the state" and "against betrayal of the German people and treasonable subversion." The Communist deputies and functionaries were arrested, the Communist and Social Democratic press suspended. Hitler translated into fact what he had proclaimed from the start: "Once we are in power, we shall, as God lives, hold on to it. No one shall take it away from us."

However, even in the parliamentary elections, the Nazis polled only 43.9 per cent of the vote. Lacking a clear majority, they continued to depend on their coalition with the Nationalists.

On March 23, Hitler placed before Parliament the draft of a "Law for Abolishing the Distress of People and Reich," the so-called "Enabling Act." It was approved by 441 votes against 94 Social

Democratic votes. It gave Hitler full legislative powers for the next four years. He now combined in his person executive and legislative authority.

Hitler immediately proceeded to misuse the unlimited powers conferred upon him by the majority of the deputies. In the course of one year he eliminated the Social Democratic party, its functionaries following the previously purged Communists into concentration camps. The middle-class parties realized too late what it meant to give Hitler full power. They either resigned and announced their dissolution or were suspended by decree. By the end of 1933, the only surviving party was the Nazi Party, elevated by Hitler on December 1 to the status of Party of the State.

But trouble was brewing within the party itself, in the so-called "Brown Shirt" army, the S.A. In 1933 it numbered two million men and clamored for recognition of its contribution during the years of struggle. Started by Hitler in 1921 as his bodyguard at rallies, the Brown Shirts had contributed decisively to his victory. They had intimidated the Democrats, fought physically with the Communists in the so-called beer-hall battles, and paid for their victories with numerous dead. Their chief, Ernst Röhm, a former Army officer and Hitler's supporter from earliest days, demanded that the official German Army, the Reichswehr, be replaced by the brown militia. But Hitler had decided for the Army and against the S.A. To the public and to President Hindenburg he pretended that the S.A. was preparing a revolt against the state; he arrested Röhm and the chief S.A. functionaries on June 30, 1934, and had them executed by the S.S. without trial. He also used that occasion to eliminate some of his opponents and party renegades, justifying these murders retroactively by decreeing, on July 3, 1934, the law of "Self-Defense of the State." From then on the S.A. was relegated to the role of an athletic league within the party. The victor of June 30, 1934, was the S.S., whose chief, Heinrich Himmler, now took over the administration of the political police in all German states, and the establishment of a network of concentration camps.

41 / Hitler in happy mood

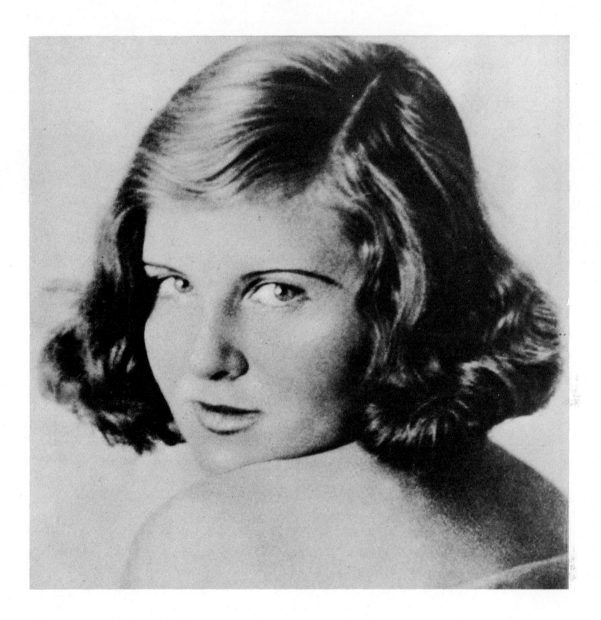

42 / Eva Braun, the daughter of a trade-school teacher in Munich,
who became Hitler's mistress after the death of
Hitler's niece Geli Raubal

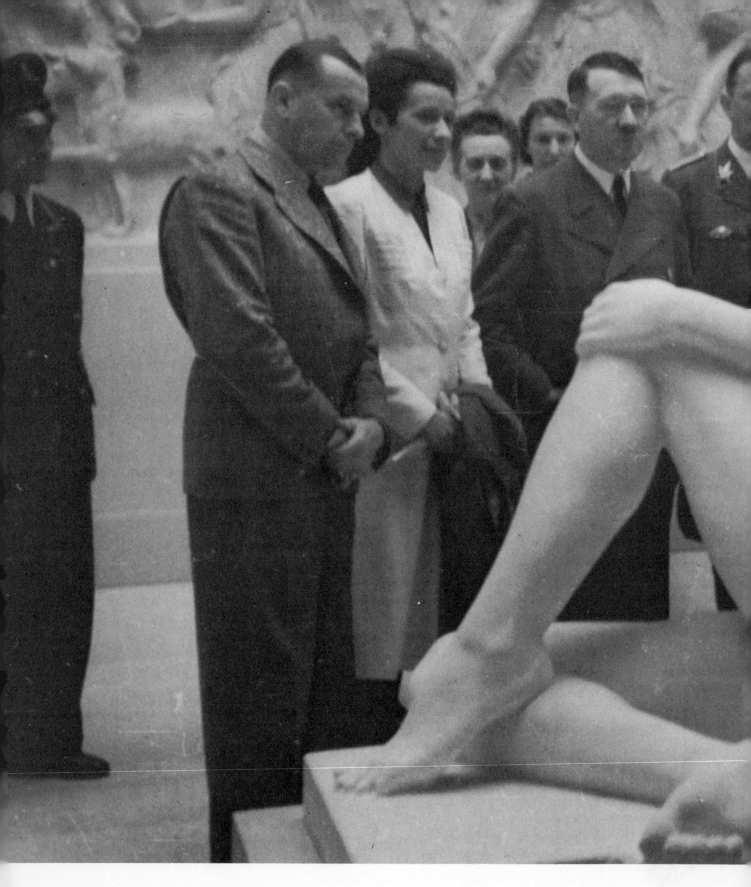

43 / Hitler at an art exhibition

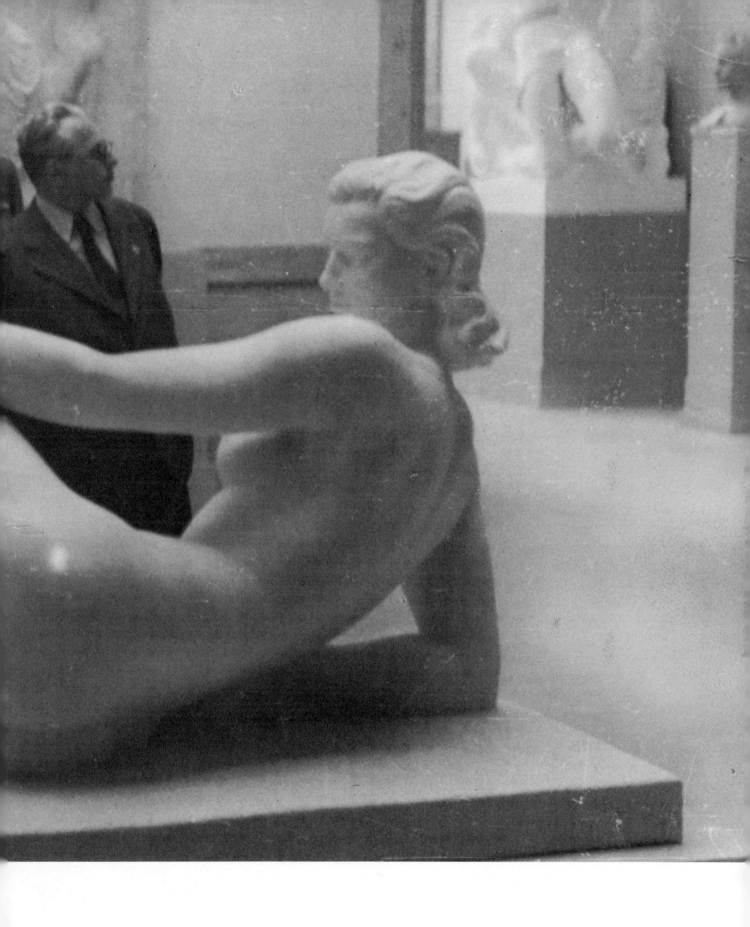

On the following two pages:

44 / Hitler and S.A. Chief of Staff Ernst Röhm
at the 1933 Nuremberg "Victory Party Rally"

45 / 1935: Hitler, Frau Goebbels, and Goebbels in the Chancellery gardens

46 / 1936:
Hitler at the
harvest thanksgiving
on the Bückeberg,
hailed by
German peasants,
and
guarded by the S.S.

47 / Minister of the Air Force Göring distributing photographs of Hitler

At right:

48 / The Chancellor on a trip,
carrying a horse whip for personal protection

49 / Members of the
League of German Girls
line up
at the Obersalzberg
to greet Hitler

HITLER
FACES OF
A DICTATOR

50 / Hitler at his eyrie, the Berghof, on the Obersalzberg,
a place of pilgrimage for the party. Here, Hitler sought relaxation

President Hindenburg died on August 2, 1934. On the day preceding his death, a law was enacted combining the offices of Chancellor and President, which was ratified by a plebiscite that gave Hitler 89.9 per cent of the vote. As "Führer and Reich Chancellor" he was also Commander in Chief of the Armed Forces and held powers unequaled by any German statesman before him. Unhampered by opposition, he was able to pursue the goal he had presented to the military commanders three days after his appointment as Chancellor: Following the rebuilding of Germany's military forces, "living space in the East" was to be conquered, which would then be "ruthlessly Germanized."

The politically unsophisticated German people, whom Hitler contemptuously referred to as "the masses," believed that Hitler had brought them peace and order. He gave them work and bread. The economy was stimulated by public works and commissions, chiefly in the armament industry. Unemployment, already decreasing as the Depression receded, diminished still further through Hitler's "Program of Job Creation."

On March 7, 1936, Hitler astounded the world by the following proclamation: "In the interests of the basic rights of a people to secure its borders and to guarantee its defense, the German government, as of today, has restored the unrestricted sovereignty of the Reich." Early in the morning, German troops entered the demilitarized zone of the Rhineland. After having declared Germany's withdrawal from the disarmament conference and the League of Nations in the autumn of 1933, Hitler now repudiated the Locarno Pact also.

The international reaction to this breach of treaties was as feeble as it had been when, on March 9, 1935, Hitler had announced the rebuilding of the German Air Force, and on March 16 the re-establishment of universal military service, in violation of the Versailles Peace Treaty. On May 21, 1935, Hitler treated the

Parliament in Berlin and the world at large to his "Thirteen-Point Peace Speech," in which he declared that he had no more fervent wish than everlasting peace for Germany and the world. He had re-established the German military position only in order to make Germany a partner with equal rights. Within the circle of his party friends, however, he betrayed his true intentions in a discussion of the education of German youth: "My educational principles are harsh. Every weakness has to be hammered away. In my fortress castles [training schools for the Nazi elite] young men will be trained who will make the world tremble. I want a violent, arrogant, fearless youth. . . . With them I will create a new world. . . . By the harshest tests, they shall learn to master the fear of death. This is the stage of heroic young men."

In March, 1938, Hitler set his armed forces in motion for the second time. He "joined" his native Austria to Germany. On April 10, in a national plebiscite, the Austrian vote—99.73 per cent of the Austrian population—endorsed Hitler's action. In the same year he pursued "the solution of the Sudeten Question"—the German minority living within the borders of Czechoslovakia. He declared that, once the Sudeten territories were ceded to Germany, the last of Germany's territorial claims would be settled. At the Munich Conference of September 29, 1938, England, France, and Italy endorsed the cession. England's Prime Minister, Neville Chamberlain, proclaimed on his return to London: "I bring you peace in our time." Chamberlain evidently was unacquainted with Hitler's *Mein Kampf,* in which Hitler had stated as early as 1924: "When the Reich embraces within its borders every single German but is unable to offer him the means of subsistence, then the distress of one's own people establishes the moral justification for the conquest of foreign territory. The plow then becomes the sword, and from the tears of war grows the bread of future generations."

Chamberlain knew only Hitler's statement: ". . . we don't want any Czechs! The Sudeten territory is our last territorial claim in Europe!"

Six months later, in violation of the Munich agreement, Hitler forced the Czech President, Dr. Emil Hácha, to acquiesce in the occupation of his country. The remnants of Czechoslovakia, now designated as the Protectorate of Bohemia and Moravia, were taken into German custody. For the first time, Hitler took the risk of war.

51 / At the Obersalzberg. Hitler with a tame jackdaw

52 / Hitler and female visitors at the Berghof

53 / 1934: Anthony Eden and British Foreign Minister Sir John Simon (*left*)
call on Hitler at the Chancellery in Berlin.
At right, his interpreter Paul Schmidt, Minister of Foreign Affairs von Neurath,

and the British ambassador, Sir Eric Phipps. Von Ribbentrop,
his back to the camera, was Neurath's successor as Minister
of Foreign Affairs from 1938

54 / Baldur von Schirach, leader of the National Socialist youth
organization, the Hitler Youth, at a demonstration in Nuremberg
with Hitler

At right:

55 / 1936: Adolf Hitler leaves the Nuremberg Party Congress

56 / Hitler with his
closest collaborators
Front row from left:
Minister of Labor
Franz Seldte;
Hitler's Deputy
Rudolf Hess;
Minister of the Interior
Dr. Wilhelm Frick;
Martin Bormann,
and Chief of Staff
of the S.A.
Viktor Lutze

57 / Hitler in his
Reich Chancellery
apartment
in Berlin

Hitler receives foreign guests on the Obersalzberg:

Above:

59 / The Duke of Windsor, formerly King Edward VIII, and the Duchess of Windsor

At left:

58 / Former British Prime Minister Lloyd George, Ribbentrop in the background, *left*, interpreter Schmidt between Hitler and Lloyd George

An den Fuehrer und Reichskanzler.

Beim Verlassen Deutschlands danken die Herzogin
von Windsor und ich Ihnen aufrichtig fuer die grosse
Gastfreundschaft, die Sie uns gewaehrt haben und fuer
die vielen Moeglichkeiten, das zu sehen, was fuer das
Wohl der schaffenden Deutschen getan wird.

Wir nehmen einen tiefen Eindruck von unserer Reise
durch Deutschland mit und werden nie vergessen, mit
welcher Aufmerksamkeit wir von Ihren Beauftragten um-
geben worden sind, und eine wie herzliche Aufnahme wir
ueberall gefunden haben.

Besonders danken wir Ihnen fuer die schoenen
Stunden, die wir mit Ihnen auf dem Obersalzberg ver-
bracht haben.

                              EDWARD

                    23-X-37

From the day of Hitler's assumption of power, National Socialist Germany developed into a military camp. Virtually every German had to enlist in one of the many party organizations to be trained for some national purpose. Hitler's goal was to shape the Germans into a strongly knit patriotic whole with the single aim of serving him and the Reich in a spirit of total self-sacrifice. Those who stood aside were mercilessly persecuted and branded as traitors incapable of understanding "the greatness of the new era."

Hitler in 1938: "These young people now learn nothing but how to think German, how to act German; these ten-year-olds enter our Young Folk and there for the first time feel and breathe a fresh breeze; then, four years later, they graduate from the Young Folk to the Hitler Youth and there we keep them another four years.

"After that we don't think of releasing them into the hands of our old fosterers of class prejudice, but take them immediately into the party, the Labor Front, the S.A. or the NSKK [National Socialist Kraftfahr Korps]. And if they have been there for two years or eighteen months and still aren't wholehearted National Socialists, we put them into the Labor Service and give them another six months' going-over . . . and what's left of caste arrogance after those six or seven months will be taken care of by the military in the next two years.

"And when they come back after two, three, or four years, we take them right back into the S.A., the S.S., and so on, to keep them from backsliding, and they won't ever be free for the rest of their lives. And if someone tells me there'll always be dissenters, I answer: 'National Socialism is not at the end of its day, but at its very beginning.' "

Germany's citizens were trapped in the network of Nazi organizations: easy to supervise, easy to manipulate, and easily misused.

On November 7, 1938, a young Polish Jew, Herschel Grynszpan, shot and killed Ernst vom Rath, a young secretary at the German

Embassy in Paris, in an act of desperate protest. Members of the Nazi organizations reacted promptly under orders: throughout Germany, synagogues were set afire, Jewish shops were demolished, 26,000 Jews were arrested, mistreated, and put into concentration camps. With the "Night of the Broken Glass" the persecution of the Jews reached its first climax.

The persecution had started as early as April 1, 1933, with a day of boycott against Jewish businessmen, professors, teachers, students, school children, lawyers, and physicians. What had been set down by Hitler in 1924 in *Mein Kampf* he now translated into action: "I believe that I act today in unison with the Almighty Creator's intention: by fighting the Jews, I do battle for the Lord." On September 15, 1935, at the Nuremberg Reich Party Day, he put before the National Socialist deputies—there now were no others—the "Reich Citizen Law" and the "Law for the Protection of German Blood and Honor." The deputies adopted these laws without objection, and about 500,000 Jewish citizens were expelled from the national community.

It was the success of the "Night of the Broken Glass" in 1938 which encouraged Hitler to envisage the "Final Solution," and the war gave him the opportunity to put it into action.

By the end of the war, about four million European Jews had been exterminated in the gas chambers of Auschwitz, Majdanek, and Treblinka. No registers were kept of the Jews killed in Polish ghettos and in Russia. Their number is estimated at several millions.

61 / Hitler with his half-sister and housekeeper Angela Raubal

On the following two pages:

62 / March 1938: On his entry into Austria,
Hitler is greeted by one of his former teachers

63 / 1940:
Hitler with Mussolini

64 / March 1939: Signing the edict establishing
the Protectorate of Bohemia and Moravia,
Hitler wears glasses. He forbade publication
of the photograph and canceled the negative
by crossing it out

At right, above:

65 / Hitler with Czechoslovakia's
President Dr. Hácha

At right, below:

66 / Hitler passing before an
honor guard at the Hradčany Castle
in Prague,
after the German occupation of
Czechoslovakia

67 / 1939: Minister
of Foreign Affairs
Ribbentrop
reporting to
Hitler
after signature
of the
German-Soviet
nonaggression treaty
in Moscow,
August 23

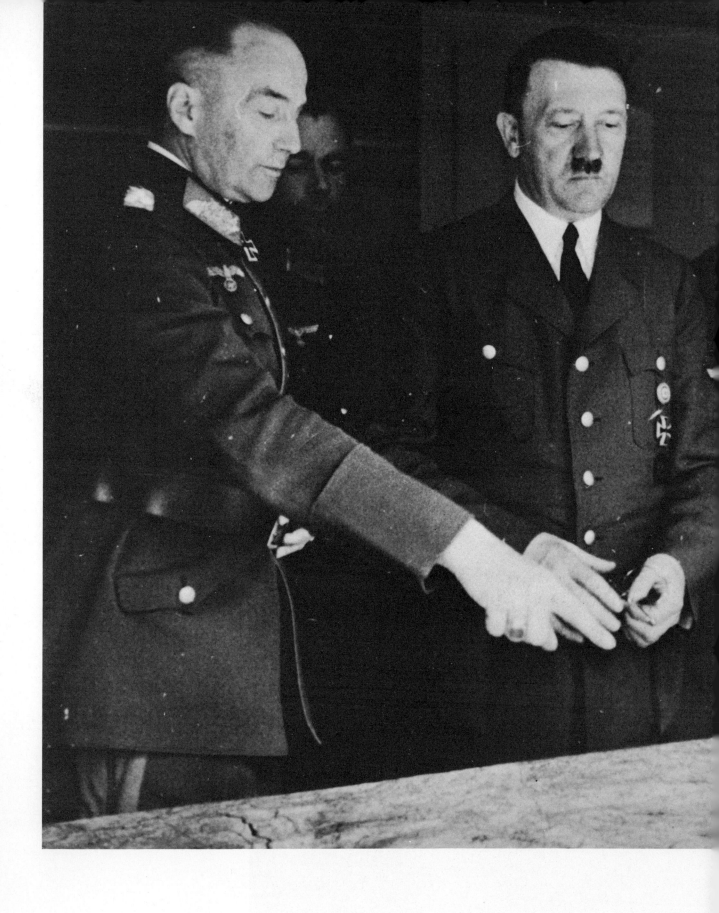

68 / Hitler with Army Commander in Chief von Brauchitsch at a military
conference during the French campaign

69 / Twenty-five years earlier:

Above:

1914 (*front row, left*) Hitler as soldier in World War I

At right:

1916 (*upper row, right*) Hitler in the field hospital at Beelitz,
recuperating from a shrapnel injury

On November 10, 1938, Hitler instructed the German press to prepare the people for war. "Circumstances forced me to speak for decades of virtually nothing but peace. Only by constantly stressing Germany's desire for peace and its peaceful intentions was I able to regain, bit by bit, freedom for the German people and to give them the armament required for each consecutive step. It is obvious that such peace propaganda, prolonged over a number of years, must have undesirable effects; it may easily establish in a great many minds the fixed idea that the present regime is synonymous with the decision and the will to keep peace under any circumstances. This, however, would not only lead to a mistaken evaluation of the aims of our system, but above all it would fail to inspire the German nation with a steadfast facing of events, and eventually lead to a spirit of defeatism destructive for the successes of the German government. . . ."

Hitler wanted to prepare the German people "to remain steadfast, even if lightning and thunder are starting."

The first thunderclouds appeared when he annexed truncated Czechoslovakia. This violation of the Rights of Nations upset the signatories of the Munich agreement, but did not provoke military intervention. Chamberlain, who had deluded himself that he was the bringer of "peace in our time," revised his politics.

On his initiative, France and England gave Poland, the country whose turn would evidently be next, a guarantee of support. This in no way discouraged Hitler. Reiterating his wish for peace, he spoke of an untenable state of affairs at Germany's eastern border, demanded that Danzig revert to the Reich and East Prussia and Danzig be connected with Germany by a railway and a superhighway with extraterritorial status across the Polish Corridor. Poland refused these demands. On August 23, 1939, Hitler concluded a friendship pact with Stalin, his chief ideological opponent, in an attempt to outmaneuver Poland's Western allies and to isolate Poland.

On September 1, 1939, at 4:45 in the morning, German troops marched into Poland; England and France kept their promise of support and two days later declared war on Germany. The Second World War had begun.

Poland was quickly overrun by the Germans, Stalin and Hitler sharing the booty.

Hitler declared to the chiefs of the Armed Forces: "Nobody has achieved what I have achieved. My life is no longer what matters. I have led the German people to great heights, even if today the whole world hates us. I have to choose between victory or annihilation. I choose victory."

As soon as the Polish campaign was concluded, Hitler ordered the Army to the French border. The attack against the West, originally planned for November, 1939, was postponed to spring.

In the spring of 1940, fearful that England and France might occupy Norway, cut Germany off from its supply of Swedish iron ore, and establish control over the North Sea and the Baltic, Hitler occupied Norway and Denmark. On May 10, the Norwegian action not quite completed, he attacked in the West. Disregarding the neutrality of Holland, Belgium, and Luxemburg, he occupied these countries also, and from there invaded France. Six weeks later, on June 22, the French surrendered and the armistice was signed in the Forest of Compiègne.

The National Socialist press hailed Hitler as "the greatest military leader of all times," and, with three successful campaigns behind him, the vast majority of Germans were willing to share this belief.

70 / 1940:
The conqueror of
France
visits his
soldiers

71 / Hitler and Hermann Göring, now "Marshal of the Reich"

On the following two pages:

72 / Weapon inspection

73 / 1941: Mussolini and Hitler on their way to Headquarters

74 / Hitler on one of
his visits
to the front lines

76 / Workmen in the
armament industry
pay their respects
to Hitler
at the
Reich Chancellery

78 / Hitler planning buildings
for peacetime
which never materialized

79 / Hitler and Göring

At left:

77 / Hitler observing the demonstration of new weapons. The civilian
next to him is the industrialist Hermann Röchling,
war economy chief; to his left, General Jodl

Twelve days before the end of the French campaign, on June 10, 1940, Benito Mussolini entered the war as Hitler's ally. Italy's Fascist dictator, who had successfully mediated in the Sudeten affair, had again offered Hitler his mediation in the last days before the outbreak of the Second World War. He believed that the conflict with Poland might also be settled through negotiation. Hitler, however, was not interested in this kind of solution and had refused Mussolini's intervention. Mussolini, in turn, had declared Italy a nonparticipant in the war. Now he came to realize that his country was being sidestepped by events.

In August, 1940, Mussolini began his own war, attacking the neighboring English colonies from Abyssinia. But instead of easing Hitler's war load by diverting English forces, he soon got into difficulties and had to ask the Germans for assistance. On March 31, 1941, General Erwin Rommel with his Afrika Korps intervened in the battles along the Libyan coast, the English retreated to El Alamein, but by then the strength of the German forces on this front was exhausted.

Shortly after the victory in France, Hitler relinquished his plan to invade England, hoping for an arrangement with the "Germanic brother nation." Instead he decided to attack the Soviet Union. He had planned his attack for spring, 1941, but postponed it because Mussolini, on October 28, 1940, suddenly decided to invade Greece. In April, 1941, the Germans had to come to the rescue of the Italians there; and since Yugoslavia had just established an anti-German government, Hitler subjected both Yugoslavia and Greece to a Blitzkrieg.

All this delayed the offensive against the Soviet Union, which was launched on June 22, 1941. But in Russia, the blitz techniques did not work. The vastness of the country eroded the German forces. They reached the vicinity of Moscow in the winter, but insufficient equipment and supply difficulties forced a retreat.

With sublime disregard for the extremely heavy casualties in Russia, Hitler ordered a new offensive in the south in 1942. By August, German troops had reached the Caucasus and the Volga. But on November 19 the Soviet Army launched a massive counterattack in the Stalingrad sector, encircling the Sixth German Army. Its commander in chief, Field Marshal Friedrich Paulus, surrendered on January 31, 1943. Of the 284,000 soldiers originally constituting the army, 34,000 were taken prisoners.

Three months later, the German Expeditionary Corps in Africa and the allied Italian forces had to surrender; 252,000 Germans and Italians were taken captive. On July 10, 1943, American and English forces invaded Sicily and began the conquest of Italy.

The German Armed Forces were now in retreat on all fronts. Hitler continued to pretend optimism: "I am firmly convinced that this battle will have exactly the same issue as the battle I once had to fight inside Germany." On June 6, 1944, Allied troops landed in France. At a military conference in Metz, the German generals put pressure on Hitler to cease a hopeless fight against the overwhelming superiority of the enemy. His answer echoed a statement he had made a few days before he became Chancellor of the Reich in January, 1933: "I too can be wrong and make mistakes, but what matters is who, in the end, has made the fewest mistakes. I have chosen this task because I never in my life could have chosen anything else, nor will I choose anything else; for me, it is evident that this is my life's achievement, with which I either rise or fall."

On July 20, 1944, Lieutenant Colonel Klaus Graf Schenk von Stauffenberg made an attempt to kill Hitler; he and a group of German patriots wanted to save the people and the state from total annihilation. The plot miscarried. Hitler escaped virtually unharmed. Stauffenberg was shot; many of his co-conspirators were hanged.

80 / Hitler and Bormann
inspecting models of
emergency housing
for victims of bombing

81 / Hitler
scanning photos
brought him
by a tank crew
from the front

82 / Hitler posing for his personal photographer, Heinrich Hoffmann

83 / A morning constitutional at the Rastenburg Headquarters. Hitler training his shepherd dog Blondi

84 / Hitler and Eva Braun

Above:

After the assumption of power

At right:

During the war

85 / Spring 1944: Hitler is shown new Army uniforms
Center of photo: Next to Hitler, Field Marshal Wilhelm Keitel,
subsequently executed in Nuremberg

On the following two pages:

86 / July 20, 1944: Radio address of Admiral of the Fleet Dönitz after the assassination
attempt at Headquarters. Dönitz became Hitler's successor as President of the Republic.
At the Nuremberg trial he was sentenced to ten years' imprisonment.
From bottom: Press chief Otto Dietrich; Martin Bormann; Hitler;
Jodl (with head bandaged); Hitler's aide Schaub (sitting against the wall);
the men standing against the wall are orderlies

88 / Hitler shaken by the assassination attempt

At left:

87 / Hitler and his staff after the assassination attempt.
Behind Hitler, who had suffered only minor injuries,
Martin Bormann. General Jodl, with bandaged head

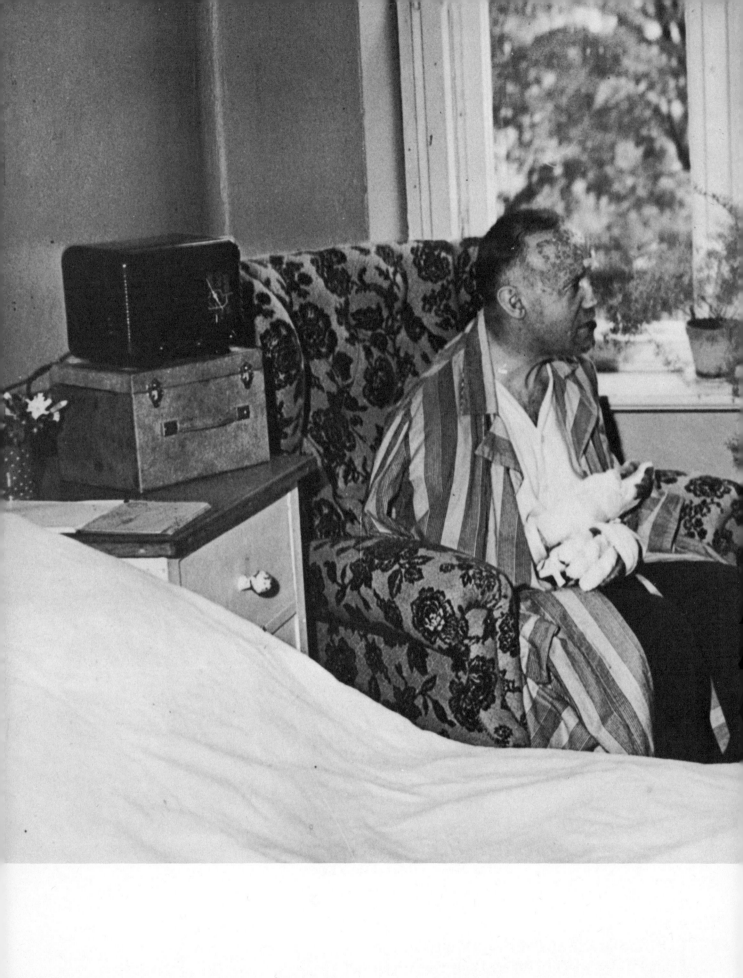

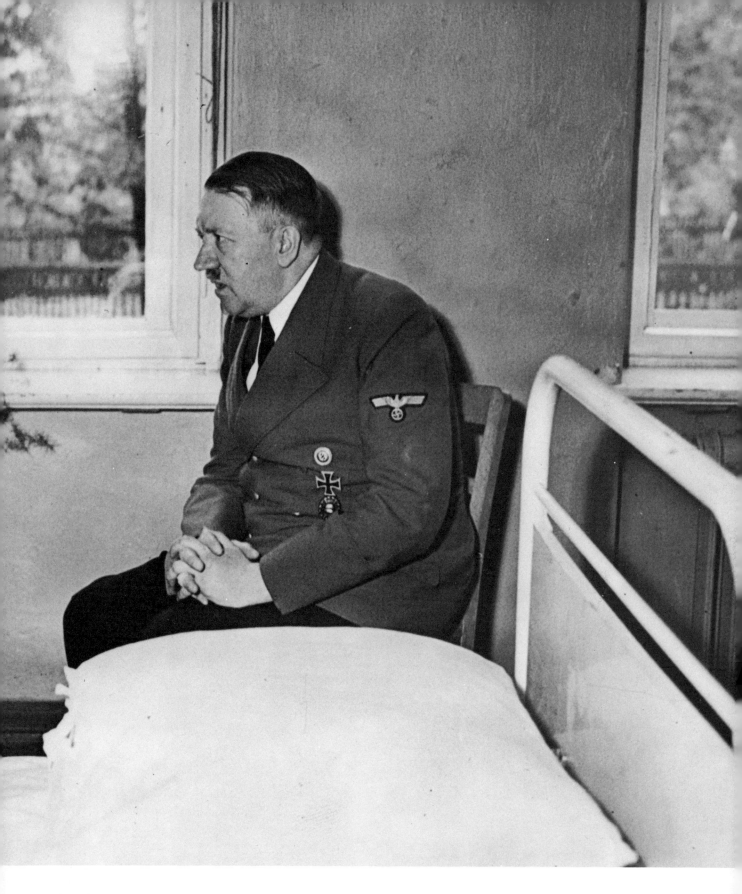

89 / Hitler visiting the severely wounded General Scherff

90 / Hitler
pointing out
his own injury to
General Scherff

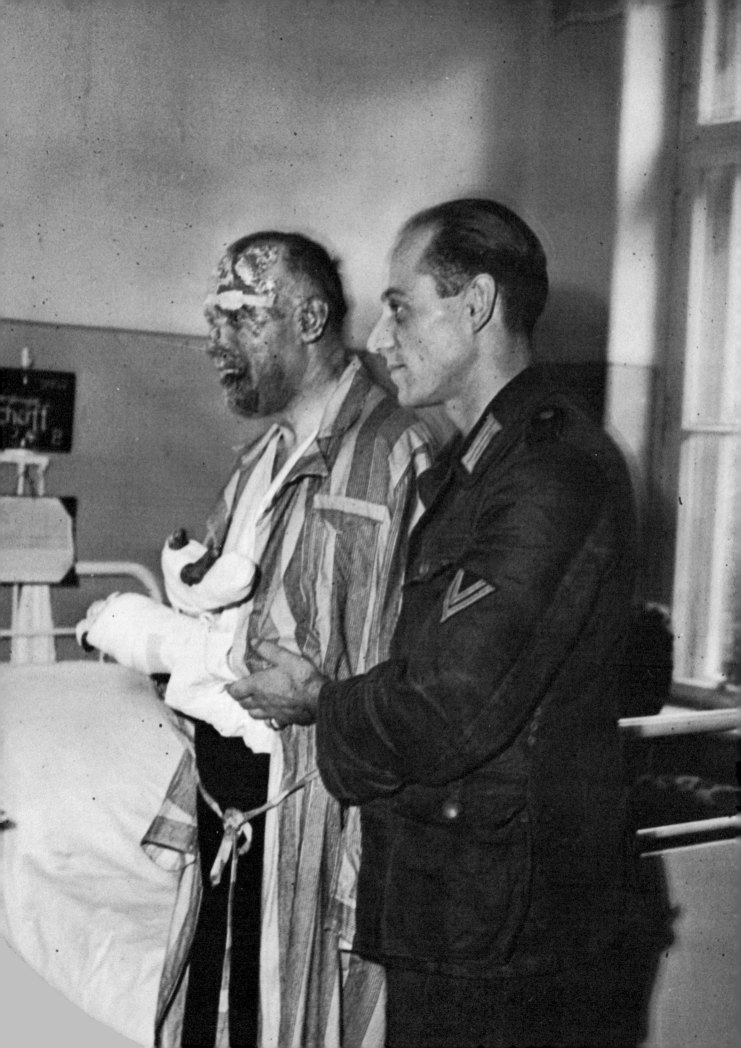

In the autumn of 1944, Hitler scraped the bottom of Germany's man power. All able-bodied men aged from sixteen to sixty were called to arms.

In early December he decided on an offensive in the West. When his Chief of Staff, General Heinz Guderian, warned against it, pointing to the dangerous situation in the East, Hitler responded furiously: "I don't need your advice! I have directed the German field armies over five years and my practical experience is much more extensive than yours. . . . I am better informed than you are."

On December 12, 1944, Hitler told his generals: "In the last analysis, wars come to a conclusion because one party or the other realizes that victory is out of reach. Every moment must be used to show the enemy that no matter what he does he cannot count on surrender. Never, never!"

Four days later, the Ardennes offensive was started. It miscarried, but it postponed the collapse of the Reich for another brief period.

On March 7, Cologne was captured, on the 29th Frankfurt am Main; and Nuremberg, "City of the Reich Party Day," fell to the Americans on April 20, 1945—Hitler's fifty-sixth birthday.

From the Oder River, the Russians began their attack on Berlin on April 16. A week later the city was encircled. In his last hours, while the Red Army was entering Berlin, Hitler married his mistress of long standing, Eva Braun. At 4:00 on the morning of April 29, he signed his last will. It fell into the hands of the Allies, who kept it secret from the Germans for a time. It was feared that even at this late date they might believe in Hitler's assurances that he was not guilty of having started the war: "It is untrue that I or anybody else in Germany wanted war in 1939. It was willed and provoked exclusively by those international statesmen who either were of Jewish extraction or worked for Jewish interests.

"I have made too many offers for the limitation and control of armaments which posterity will not be able to disregard for all time, for responsibility for the outbreak of the war to be pinned on me.

"Further, I never wished that after the first disastrous world war there should be another against England or worse still against America. Centuries will go by, but from the ruins of our cities and monuments the hatred of the ultimately responsible people will forever rise anew; they are the ones whom we have to thank for all this: international Jewry and its helpers."

In his last will Hitler also justified his massacre of the Jews in his own way: " . . . I left no doubt that, should the nations of Europe again be regarded as bundles of shares belonging to these international money and finance conspirators, then this people also would have to stand trial, this people ultimately responsible for the murderous struggle: Jewry! I made it abundantly clear that this time not only millions of children of European, Aryan origin would have to starve, not only millions of adult men would have to die, not only hundreds of thousands of women and children would be burned in the cities and bombed to extinction, but that also the ultimately guilty would have to pay for their guilt, though by more humane methods."

On April 30, at 3:30 in the afternoon, Adolf and Eva Hitler committed suicide. In front of the bunker of the Chancellery, Hitler's last headquarters, their corpses were partially burned, buried, and later disinterred by the Russians. There is no tomb.

Only Hitler's name has survived. Once, in 1932, he said in Munich: "In my last will it is stipulated that my tombstone shall be inscribed with nothing but Adolf Hitler. My title I created in my name."

In the presence of representatives of all the victorious powers, the representatives of the German Armed Forces signed the unconditional surrender on May 9, 1945, in the headquarters of Marshal Zhukov in Berlin-Karlshorst.

Adolf Hitler's Reich, the "Thousand-Year Reich," as he called it, had lasted twelve years, three months, and ten days.

91 / 1943:
Heinrich Himmler,
"Reich Leader
of the S.S."
(with spectacles),
and
Army Chief of Staff
General Zeitzler
inspect
Russian railway
installations
destroyed
on Hitler's orders

92 / 1943:
Hitler receiving
military reports
at the
Berghof

On the following two pages:

93 / Autumn 1944:
One of Hitler's
last visits
to the front.
Next to him,
his pilot,
Baur

94 / At the Berghof,
for the last time

95 / On March 20, 1945, at the Berlin Chancellery,
Hitler confers the Iron Cross for bravery in battle on a number
of Hitler youths, called to arms as a last desperate measure

96 / April 20, 1943:
Hitler
and Eva Braun,
celebrating
Hitler's fifty-fourth
birthday
on the Obersalzberg